Boris Pasternak's earliest
1912. By 1917 his third vol
being received with wild en
collection of his poems in
they were, as Lydia Sla
models, the unmistakable roots, from which modern
Russian poetry is growing'. This selection, drawn
from every period of his life, includes many of his
last poems, and some that had never appeared in
English before. Mrs Slater, who has translated them,
could scarcely be better equipped for her work. As
Pasternak's younger sister, she shared his upbringing
and background, and gained a deep understanding
of his poetry. As a poet in her own right, who has
lived in England since 1935, she is able to re-create
in English the very cadence of the original.

ACKNOWLEDGMENTS

Seventeen of the later poems in this collection appeared in *Poems by Boris Pasternak* in 1958. I should like to thank the publisher, Peter Russell, for permission to reprint them. Similar kind thanks are also due to the following journals: the *Times Literary Supplement, Unicorn, Arena*, and *Hudson Review*.

This Unwin Paperbacks edition includes a number of new poems chosen and translated by Lydia Pasternak Slater.

Poems of
Boris Pasternak

Translated by
LYDIA PASTERNAK SLATER

London
UNWIN PAPERBACKS
Boston   Sydney

First published as 'Fifty Poems' by George Allen & Unwin
in paperback 1963
Reprinted twice.
This new edition first published in Unwin Paperbacks 1984

UNWIN® PAPERBACKS
40 Museum Street, London WC1A 1LU, UK

Unwin Paperbacks
Park Lane, Hemel Hempstead, Herts HP2 4TE, UK

George Allen & Unwin Australia Pty Ltd
8 Napier Street, North Sydney, NSW 2060, Australia

British Library Cataloguing in Publication Data

Pasternak, Boris
   Poems.
I. Title
891.71'42   PG3476.P27
ISBN 0–04–891052–X

Set in 10 on 11 point Plantin
and printed in Great Britain by
Guernsey Press Co. Ltd., Guernsey, Channel Islands

CONTENTS

INTRODUCTION

by

Lydia Pasternak Slater

In the first cold and hungry years after the Revolution, whenever the necessity arose for heavy manual work, be it the rare and happy occasion of having to carry a whole sack of frozen potatoes home from work, or sawing large beams from a demolished house for firewood, or fetching a sledge with country produce from a nearby village, it was usually Boris and I who undertook the job. Once, after particularly heavy snowfalls during one of the early post-Revolutionary winters, when transport was at a standstill and trainload upon trainload of essential goods were stuck at the approaches to Moscow, the government issued a decree mobilising the non-employed population to clear the tracks. I had not yet reached the mobilisation age, but jumped at the possibility of replacing my sister, slightly older but less robust than I. In the early hours of a dark-grey winter morning, our little group met in the street with similar dejected-looking parties from other houses, and together we were marched off through the still-empty streets to the far approaches of the town. We were a sorry sight, mostly ageing members of the former intelligentsia, thin, pale, tired and unsuitably clad for the job, shuffling wearily through the dirty snow; it seemed that we would never reach our destination. When we did reach it, the sun had come out, the sky was blue and limitless, the untouched snowdrifts blindingly bright, and the air jubilant and fresh. We were allotted picks and spades and shown where and how to shovel.

To me it was like a wonderful ski-outing, but still more satisfying, as it achieved a useful purpose. I could not understand how the others could remain gloomy, and grumble in all this magnificence of nature and work. What Boris felt about it all is vividly described in one of the best chapters of 'Dr. Zhivago': the clearing of the railway-tracks during the winter journey of the Zhivagos to Siberia.

There are many other instances in this novel which remind me of a shared experience of one kind or another. But while physical exertion and concrete down-to-earth matters brought me during my adolescence into close contact with Boris, it was my sister who used to share his more abstract and intellectual interests. More serious, widely read, and with a clear and original mind leaning to philosophy and mathematics, she was an eager and welcome listener to his exciting discourses, and her opinions of his early poems carried weight with him when she was barely 12 years old. At that time, fond though I was of both my brothers, half a generation my seniors, I felt rather shy of them; and if in the course of years I grew bold enough to fight and wrestle with Alexander, Boris always inspired in me tremendous respect and awe, bordering on terror, when, on occasion, he dared to disobey the parents or to contradict them outright, which was something close to blasphemy in my childish eyes. I felt sure that he could not help despising us and our silly school-friends, yet it was nothing but his own shyness that made him appear haughty, boorish and rude, if he happened to meet them; and on the rare occasions when we did get together for any length of time, he proved to be the most generous and gentlest of brothers.

When I now try to conjure up a definite picture of him, I see him either sitting, in later years, at his table, working, muffled up in woolly pullovers, with *valenki* on his feet, the samovar singing in front of him, and a glass of very strong tea at his elbow. He would keep filling it up, continually drinking as he wrote. Or – crouching in front of the Dutch stove, pedantically stoking the log fire, not letting anyone interfere with it; or, stepping softly and unhurriedly, carefully carrying a shovelful of hot coals from one stove to another, and then methodically sweeping up the scattered bits; I remember him thus burning his beloved *valenki*. Or – long, long ago, when I was still quite small, I see him improvising at the piano late in the evening, filling the dusk with unspeakable sadness and longing. Rolling waves, a whole world of the unknown, with its terrors of love and separation, of poetry and death, emerged from under his fingers; Boris ceased to be our brother, and became something unfathomable, tremendous, a demon, a genius. We used to cry our eyes out, praying to God that he might return to earth again. In those days he did return eventually, after we had fallen asleep . . .

As the son of two artists, an impressionist painter and a great musician, he has inherited and incorporated in his poetry both visual art and music; and the music, I think, not only plays the more important part in his poetry – it *is* this poetry itself. Whenever he was inspired, excited or unhappy he invariably poured out his feelings into music, inarticulately moaning and humming as he played. It was not until much later that his music found expression in words, in poetry. He never really abandoned music, he merely changed his instrument.

The essential qualities of a musical composition are rhythm and melody. To translate my brother's poems without trying to preserve his melodies and rhythms is for me equivalent to not translating him at all.

As I pointed out in a letter to the New York Times[2], 'Pasternak, like Mayakovsky, the most revolutionary of Russian poets, has never in his life written a single line of unrhythmic poetry, and this is not because of a pedantic adherence to obsolete classical rules, but because an instinctive feeling for rhythm and harmony were inborn qualities of his genius, and he simply could not write differently.' I make it a point to do likewise.

The question of rhymes is of lesser importance, though here again it was more 'natural' for my brother to use rhymes than to write without them. All the poems included in this book were fully rhyming in the original, but in this respect I have not followed his example; I could of course claim, with many a critic and poet, that rhyming in translations is not needed and is often entirely superfluous, even at times hindering the appreciation of the poem. This may well be so, but it can also be simply a happy excuse. My main reason for not completely reproducing my brother's rhyme-patterns was the difficulty of doing so if I wanted, as indeed I did, to preserve at the same time the rhythm, the melody and the contents of a poem and avoid artificial sentence constructions.

His rhyme-patterns are in general classical, with male and

female rhymes alternating in a four-line stanza (ab ab, or occasionally ab ba), but he also uses double couplets (aa bb), as in 'The Zoo', or sonnets, or altogether different, complicated patterns. Occasionally there is a repetition of the same ba pattern throughout a whole poem, so that there are about a dozen lines, ending in words all rhyming with one another, alternating with another dozen different line-endings also sounding alike. I regret that I could not reproduce exactly the interesting and very effective rhyme-pattern of the 'Thunderstorm, instantaneous forever', where not lines within a stanza but corresponding lines in successive stanzas rhyme with each other, as follows: abcd abcd efgh efgh, and where d and h are also assonances. As a rule, I have reproduced at least one set of rhymes in each stanza (in the above case rhyming the d's and the h's), in general, the rhymes of the second and fourth line. Occasionally I have succeeded in preserving the whole set of rhymes; in two instances only have I left out the rhymes altogether, in the third of the 'Three Variants' and in 'Stars were racing'.

I have tried to translate in the same way as my brother wrote. Of course I cannot claim to have produced English Pasternak poems; but I can and do claim to have given renderings in English which, when read aloud, come very close in their sound and their general pattern to those of the Russian originals.

The poems in this book have not been selected according to a well-thought-out plan, nor for any special purpose or reason. They happened to get translated more or less at random, partly because I particularly liked one poem or another, partly because this or that poem was connected with a memory of Boris himself reading it to us in Moscow at the time he wrote it, partly because one or another of them had never before been translated. On the other hand, some had been translated a number of times by different people but, dissatisfied with the result, I tried to produce a better rendering.

Had this book been planned from the start as a representative collection of my brother's work, my selection would have been a different one. For one thing, it contains many more poems written in the last years of his life than at any other period. The reason for this is not so much Boris's own preference for the maturer poetry of his last years, as the fact that at the time I received them these poems were not yet known to the public, either in the West or in Russia, and to translate them was for me an inspiring challenge.

Though not in the strictest sense a representative selection, this book does, in fact, contain examples of Pasternak's poetry from most of his publications, and I think there are, chronologically speaking, no very important omissions. No excerpts have been included, however, from his very long narrative poems 'Spektorsky', 'The High Malady', 'The year 1905' and 'Lieutenant Schmidt'. I hope to translate these long poems separately if and when I can. That there is a big gap between the poems of 'Second Birth', and those of the war years, 1941 to 1944, is not exactly the fault of the translator. As we shall see from Pasternak's letters, he had started work on his novel as early as 1934 and he continued to work on it for the next two decades with shorter or longer intervals, changing, adding, remoulding separate chapters, and even completely rewriting the whole book. At the same time, he was busy translating into Russian works by many foreign writers and poets, and especially the plays of Shakespeare. These, staged by Russian theatres, became the major source of his income in the years of political and literary purges and terror.

The first collection published by Boris Pasternak was 'Twin in the Clouds'[7], a name which he later rejected as 'stupidly pretentious'; in the edition of his poems which he prepared for publication in 1957 (but which was never published in his lifetime) he included only a few of these earliest poems, in the sub-section entitled 'Initial Period'. From these I have included 'February' and 'Venice'. I well remember the impact 'February' and some others of this period made on us when we first heard them read. This was a completely new and overwhelming experience.

From the next book 'Over the Barriers'[8], I have included six poems.

Then come nine poems from 'My Sister Life'[9] (summer 1917). This latter was, I believe, Pasternak's most celebrated book of poems, and the more sophisticated younger generation of literary Russians were particularly excited by it. There was in Russia at that time a very real contact between the poet and the public, greater than anywhere else in Europe, I think, and certainly far greater than is even imaginable in England. Books of poetry were published in enormous editions and were sold out within a few days of publication. Posters were stuck up all over the town announcing poets' gatherings, and everyone interested in poetry (and who in Russia did not belong to this category?) flocked to the lecture hall or forum to hear his favourite poet.

The wild enthusiasm of the Pasternak fans was not mass hysteria; this was something different: each reader discovered individually and for himself that these poems were the spontaneous outbursts of a genius, of a poet 'by the grace of God'. Some had sensed this already from his first two books, but 'My Sister Life' confirmed and accentuated their feeling of gratitude and happiness in an unprecedented way. The book contains hardly any poems which are not significant. True, these poems, and the earlier ones to a still greater extent, were at times obscure, difficult to interpret or indeed to grasp, and were so unusual in their revolutionary construction and paradoxical immediacy, their 'unpoetic' choice of subject matter, their incomplete sentences, assonances and half-rhymes, that it is not surprising that Pasternak's elders and betters, shocked and bewildered, and trying in vain to understand the boundless enthusiasm of his followers, were unable to see what it was all about, and were frequently annoyed by the apparent irrationality of what they read. Of course, some of these early poems really were too complicated, too cryptic, perhaps too hastily written, and had too many easy escapes into the brilliance of sound and words. Too little care had been taken to simplify them, to introduce order and precision into what they expressed. It is this that largely conditioned Boris's retreat from some of them in later years. But to deny their immediate power of revelation, their impressionist impact, or their significance for the future would be absurd. Already they have become the classic models, the unmistakable roots, from which modern Russian poetry is growing, and Pasternak's poems of the last period – the only ones he was prepared to acknowledge unconditionally – are, with all their biblical simplicity and resignation, unthinkable without these beginnings; they are still imbued with the same spirit of spontaneous freshness and youth, the same

14

brilliance of words and expressions, and the same unconscious originality.

The next book, 'Themes and Variations'[10] consolidated Pasternak's reputation as a great poet. These were among the last poems I heard him read to us in Moscow. I particularly remember the winter poems of 1918–19 of the 'Illness' series; and the facts and the atmosphere of what he wrote about have so merged in my memory with the poems themselves that I do not know any more whether it is the poems I remember or the actual winter nights, the Kremlin in continual snowstorms, the booming sound of the bell from the church of Ivan the Great on New Year's Eve, drowning in the wind, resounding, and falling again into the abyss of blizzard and snow, the nostalgia of overwhelming sadness, feverish drama, greatness and destiny. This book is represented here by six poems.

Next on my list are the children's poems[11]. 'The Zoo' and 'The Roundabouts', both probably written in the first place for his little son, are as far as I know my brother's only poems written specifically for children. They are neither typical 'children's poems' nor are they representative of Pasternak; they are refreshingly simple, unconventional and quietly humorous snapshots from a short visit to the zoo and a day at the fair. I translated them because they were quite new to me and had, as far as I could ascertain, never before been translated into English, or any other language for that matter. Even in the original Russian they had not been published outside Russia until 1960, when they appeared in the University of Michigan edition[12].

I faintly remember another 'children's' work by my brother, a commissioned fairy tale, which was as involved and fascinating as E. T. A. Hoffmann's fairy tales, and equally unsuitable for children. It got lost, with some other writings of my brother's, before it could be published. All I remember about it now are one or two stanzas of nostalgic poetry, sprinkled into the shadow of a plot written in prose. It had a juxtaposition of round, heated vulgarity and savageness, embodied in the Carp, alias the sun or the summer, on the one hand, and the pale blue, cool silkiness, moonlit princeliness of Naphtalène on the other. I think the Carp finally stole the prince's regalia and killed him. I suppose this tale arose out of associations with spring-cleaning, putting the winter things away into a chest with naphtalene in a kind of present-day symbolic burial ritual. As so often with Pasternak, the plot did not really matter; what mattered was the beauty of the poetic lines, notably those on Naphtalène's funeral.

Next come six poems of the years 1930–32, from 'Mixed Poems' and from the section 'Waves' of the book 'Second Birth'[13]. This was the time of Pasternak's meeting with Mrs. Z. Neuhaus, his future second wife.

From the two slim collections of poems of the war years, 'On Early Trains'[14] and 'The Vastness of Earth'[15], I have included three poems altogether.

This brings us to the last section – the poems my brother hoped to publish in 1957 under the collective name 'In the Interval'. It was to contain all the poems of Yuri Zhivago[16] under the title, 'Poems from a Novel in Prose', and the cycle, 'When It Clears Up'. As already mentioned, a substantial number of these poems are reprinted here from the previous edition of my translations[5]. To these eleven new translations have been added.

Introductions, if read at all, are very often read only after the main body of the book. It seems legitimate therefore to include here a commentary on the book as a whole as well as on its various parts. What I should most like to do is to use this space for putting right the innumerable errors and inventions of various writers and journalists who in their publications of or about Pasternak have tried to acquaint their readers with so-called facts about my brother's life, intentions and family background. There has been printed, particularly in America, such a flood of incredible 'information' about Boris Pasternak and those nearest to him – sometimes deeply wounding, sometimes trying to represent him as a sugary saint – that it seemed utterly futile to protest against even the worst offenders against fact, tact and taste. Paper is patient and so is the Pasternak family. Only twice have I been provoked into writing letters to the Editor[1, 2], and twice more have I been encouraged to revise and correct unofficially for English publishers the worst errors in books already published in the United States, though by no means all my corrections were incorporated in the new editions. An introduction to a paperback book of poetry is, moreover, not exactly a forum for polemics, nor would it be possible to deal in a few sentences with the whole mass of misrepresentation, always arrogantly ignorant, and occasionally hilariously funny. I hope one day to have enough leisure to write a book about it all, but in the meantime the most I can allow myself is an outline, at the end of this introduction, of the lives and personalities of the Pasternak parents, as it is they who have in general fared worst. I think it is unnecessary to emphasize how important a part they played in the development of Boris's own personality, or that they were indirectly responsible for his becoming the kind of poet he was. 'All I am I owe to you, in the way of inheritance, in the way of education, in the way of influence', is what Boris himself wrote in a letter to his parents, as quoted by S. Shimansky[3]. To reinforce the point I shall add some more revealing extracts from Pasternak's letters to his mother and father, before writing about our parents myself.

Extracts from Boris Pasternak's Letters to his Parents*

To his father, 1934 'I am now as old as you were in 1906 in Berlin. It is enough for me to remember you at that period to shrink back from the comparison. You were a real man . . . a Colossus, and before this image, large and wide as the world, I am a complete nonentity and in every respect still a boy as I was then, only with a broader chest and fewer teeth. . . . I have been looking through your monograph[17] again, after a long period of time, and was suddenly struck by the impact of your personality. What a wonderful artist you are! What temperament in the technique of your realism! This is what art should be, like the allegro vivace of Tchaikovsky's Sixth Symphony – let Mama remind you of it – all from beginning to end in a burst of one movement! . . . Within the limits of judgement possible in an exclamation, I think that your best subjects were Tolstoy and Josephine.† How you drew them! Your drawings of Josephine were such that she grew up according to them, followed them in her life, developed through them more than through anything else. Do you

* These letters remain the copyright of the Pasternak family.
† My elder sister.

not feel this too? What do you think of yourself and how do you feel about it? In your place, with such a life behind you, I should feel in the seventh heaven. Such a life, such a hand, such encounters and recollections!

Well, though late, I too have at last seen light. Nothing I have written so far is of any significance. That world has ceased and I have nothing to show to this new one. It would be bad if I did not understand this. But luckily I am alive, my eyes are open, and I am hurriedly trying to transform myself into a writer of a Dickensian kind, and later – if I have enough strength to do it – into a poet in the manner of Pushkin. Do not imagine that I dream of comparing myself with them! I am naming them simply to give you an idea of my inner change. In other words I have become a particle of my time and state, and their interests have become my own.'

To his parents, 1934 'How I long to see you both on such evenings, after six minutes on Barbarossa.*. . . There is no substitute, with no one else could I probably talk better and more deeply about the most important things, about life, human experience, about history, about art. . . . Sometimes it seems to me that if ever I was choosing something special in life, was working on something, if I tried to achieve, and if ever I have achieved something, then somewhere in the depths of my being I had been doing it for you. And you are not here, and for whom did I then prepare it all? . . . I am fearfully hungry for you . . .'

1936 '. . . When I was once asked for my biographical data, all I gave was data on you two – is this not axiomatic?'

1937 'What a wonderful postcard you sent me! How you calmed me with a few sentences, with your magnanimity, the youthfulness of your tone! How much you both have done for me in life, and how much you still do. But how did you know what I needed to be told!? . . . Work, to work. . . . What I wanted to say is that, although the separation from Zhenichka,† and from you,

* His parents' telephone exchange in Berlin.
† Boris's son from the first marriage.

18

means that I never will or can be really happy, I am now in the possession of the nucleus, the blinding nucleus of what one could call happiness. It is in the terribly slowly growing manuscript, which again, after an interval of years, is facing me as something substantial, lawfully increasing and spreading, as if that vegetative nervous system of mine whose upset made me so ill two years ago were looking at me in full health from its pages, and were returning from them to me. Do you remember my 'Povest'?[18] That was by comparison a decadent work. This new work is growing into something big, by much more modest but also more lasting means. I mentioned 'Povest' because what little qualities it did possess were all of an inner order. The same plastic authenticity is working here too, but with all its strength, and as I said, in a simple, more transparent form. I keep thinking of Chekhov, and the few to whom I have shown parts of it are reminded of Tolstoy. But I do not know when I shall publish it, and am not worrying about it. (And when will I have finished it?!)'

1938. 'Once again I have been looking through and touching with my fingers, down to the foundations, to the last scrap of paper, the testimony of various years, the witnesses of almost sixty years existence, if counted from the first issue of *The Artist*, which one by one have passed in order through my hands. . . . For about ten days I have been preparing alone the things for the move. I kept remembering the same kind of work in similar surroundings, but shared with Mama, during our move to this flat from the Miásnitskaya in 1911. Conditions, as well as the objects of care in both cases, are incomparable. It is as if two similar happenings occurred in two different centuries very far away from each other. . . . Your life passed before me, yours, Mama, as well as Papa's. What a feeling of pride kept overpowering me, as in all its laconic simplicity it became more and more clear to me that your life alone had taken place here, enviably deserving, honest, real, to the last shred of spirituality marked by talent, success and happy productivity; that nothing more was added to it later, that the greatest thing I could do afterwards was to preserve on some level, without soiling it, that good name which – with a fresher, broader, more significant and happier content – you left me, complete.'

19

From an Autobiographical note in 1924 'I was born in Moscow on the 29th of January 1890. Much, if not everything, I owe to my father, the Academician L. Pasternak, and to my mother, a magnificent pianist.'

'My father, the Academician L. O. Pasternak'

Biographical data and appreciations of my father's work have been published often enough after his death in catalogues and periodicals, but they usually contain grave errors of one kind or another. The most reliable information so far is in David Buckman's book, *Leonid Pasternak – a Russian Impressionist*, published in London in 1974. In Britain various examples of his work can be found in private collections as well as in the Tate gallery, the Victoria & Albert Museum, the British Museum, and various provincial galleries, but he is best represented in the Ashmolean Museum, Oxford. My father's memoirs, *Zapisi Raznykh Let*, were brought out by the Soviet publishing house *Sovietsky Khudozhnik* in Moscow in 1975, and a slightly abridged, richly illustrated English translation by Jennifer Bradshaw, with an introduction by Josephine Pasternak, was published by Quartet Books, London, in 1982.

My father knew from his earliest childhood what he wanted to do, and what he was going to be. In spite of all the discouragement he received at home, he never had the slightest doubt about his calling as an artist, and never regretted following it. I am emphasizing this point, as it has been suggested that he really longed to become a doctor, and that Yuri Zhivago was partly modelled on him – a rather absurd suggestion. True, while pursuing his art studies, first in Moscow, then in the Munich Academy, he also entered the university as a medical student, soon changing over to, and graduating in, law; but this was done solely for the sake of his parents, who, fearing the uncertainties of an artistic career, were anxious to see Leonid established in a 'respectable' profession. Of unquestionable loyalty and integrity, with an exaggerated sense of responsibility and duty, which made his personal life more austere and difficult than it need have been, my father was a man of a dreamy, gentle disposition, kind and altruistic, slow and uncertain in anything but his work, modest, retiring, and with a genuine dislike of being in the limelight, which at times it was not easy for him to avoid. He also had a wonderful sense of humour, and an ability for impersonation; observing and drawing were for him a natural necessity, like sleeping or breathing. A small drawing-pad and a pencil accompanied him always, everywhere, and one never found him sitting idle.

It was fascinating to watch him at work: when painting a portrait, he would put the easel with the picture next to, and at the level of, the sitter, and would retreat from them to the far corner of the room. From here he would observe and compare the two, completely absorbed in excited concentration, with a smile on his lips, and muttering absent-mindedly encouragement to whatever he was painting, 'That's it; yes, yes, right, let's see . . .'; then suddenly, with lightning speed, in one great leap, he would pounce on the portrait, add one or two brush strokes, and return again to his corner, to observe and compare once more. The speed, the ease and decisiveness with which he worked were truly amazing, and in direct contrast with his usual bearing. For quick decisions, for the practical side of life, for energetic initiative, there was at his side his never-failing source of strength, the throbbing heart of the family: mother.

'My mother, a magnificent pianist'

'The sacred fire was granted to her by God' is engraved on a small golden watch given to her by the students of Kiev University after one of her overwhelming recitals. The sacred fire burned in her all her life. Exceedingly timid and emotional, afflicted by nervous heart-attacks, she sensed with growing distress the approach of a thunderstorm long before it became apparent to others. It was as if she knew that one day she would be consumed by the elemental fires calling her back to the source. In autumn 1939, during a violent thunderstorm, she had a stroke; without regaining consciousness, she died a few days later, and with her death all joy and enchantment went out of our lives. Her whole being radiated enchantment and joy. Her music – but how can one describe in words what her playing was like, and what it did to the listener? Mother *was* music.

It is pointles to say it, for the reader will decide I am biassed as a daughter (though there are still some people alive who, having heard her recitals, feel the same), but in the whole of my life I have heard nobody play as she did, not even the greatest. There may be a greater virtuoso, a more brilliant performer, but no-one with deeper penetration, something indefinable which makes you burst out in tears at the first chord, at each movement, in sheer joy and ecstasy, which makes you forget yourself and everything else in the world and live only by and in these sounds while they last. Every time I listen to a great pianist on a record, on the radio, at a live concert, I am ready and longing to relive this, to be able to point out to my children: 'This is how she would have played it'. . . . But it is like the mirror's answer in *Snow White*, again and again: yes, incredible, wonderful, superb, over-whelming; but . . . not *quite* like her.

Rosa Kofmann was born in Odessa, 1867. When five years old she would hide under the piano while a cousin was having music lessons, and not move from the spot, fascinated and attentive. One day the teacher, puzzled by her persistence asked her about it, and the child triumphantly played her cousin's whole repertoire, without having had a single lesson herself.

Making her debut in a Mozart piano concerto with orchestra at the age of nine, Rosa went from one overwhelming success to another. Anton Rubinstein, who was among the first to realize the extent of her talent, sponsored several of her recitals, which cul-minated in her appearance in St. Petersburg; he insisted, too, on her going to Vienna to Prof. Leshetitsky, 'the only man in the world adequate to complete Rosa's musical education'. Even before her twentieth birthday she was appointed Professor of Music for Advanced Classes at the Odessa Conservatoire. And then she met Leonid Pasternak. Their marriage changed the whole course of her life. The cares and worries of a growing family, the desire and necessity to assist her husband, the impossibility of combining the dazzling career of a brilliant concert pianist with the busy life of a solicitous, self-effacing wife and anxious mother gradually forced her to give up her public appearances, for the sake of those dearest to her; and although she never gave up her art (our house, our lives were steeped in music) I cannot help

22

feeling that her sacrifice was too great, and that it would have been better if we had not been born. But maybe it was vindicated by the existence of Boris.

As to Boris's own biography, all he thought relevant to it is contained in his two essays 'Safe Conduct'[19] and 'An Essay in Autobiography'[20]. Anyone interested in knowing what sort of a person Pasternak was, what influenced him at various stages in his development, what he thought of art, of life, and of some of his contemporaries, is well advised to read these two essays. What he left out he obviously did not think important, correct, or necessary to include in them, and I do not intend to question his judgement. Here I will only reflect on the last three years, probably the most dramatic of his life.

The thaw of 1956, which brought with it an expectation, a possibility that *Doctor Zhivago* might be published in Russia (albeit in a modified, slightly abridged form), the delays and misunderstandings, the publication of the novel in Italy, the rocketing of Pasternak's name and fame and the hurling of them down into abysmal depths, the award of the Nobel Prize, its acceptance and rejection, the shameless way in which unscrupulous and greedy sensation-mongers exploited his name and his novel for their own ends, all this has unfortunately been too much the property of the street to need any recapitulation. That Boris's death in 1960 soon after his seventieth birthday was partly brought about by it all seems more than likely; and it is indeed less surprising that he finally gave way than that he held out as long as he did. More surprising still is the fact that visitors to Peredelkino right up to the Easter of 1960 unanimously reported on my brother's freshness, youthful looks, high spirits and good state of health, though he must have been suffering intensely all this time.

To a very great extent this triumph of spiritual happiness was due to the spontaneous expression of love and gratitude poured out to him in letters from thousands of individuals from all over the world, overwhelming, unbelievable, unsought for, and completely unexpected after decades of disappointment and frustration. Of course, these very letters greatly hindered him in his second source of happiness – his new work, which he had begun to write as soon as *Doctor Zhivago* was off his hands, with no less

23

zeal and enthusiasm. This time it was a play, a trilogy, set in a manor house around the time of the liberation of the serfs. But not only letters – streams of admirers, foreign visitors, journalists, and autograph hunters, preyed on his time, becoming not only a nuisance but also a very real potential danger to him. And when in the spring of 1959 the British Prime Minister was about to visit Moscow, Pasternak was strongly advised to take a holiday away from Peredelkino. He took this advice and went with his wife to Tiflis in Georgia to stay with their friend, the widow of the Georgian poet Tabidze of whom Pasternak had written so movingly in the last chapter of his autobiography.

This short visit to the Caucasus had a wonderful effect on my brother. The wild majestic scenery, the Georgians' love and admiration for him, the freedom, and the recollections of the happy days they both had spent in the same surroundings in the thirties, before their marriage – all this gave Pasternak new strength and a feeling of peace and fulfilment. He returned to Peredelkino happy and rejuvenated, full of hopes and energy for his growing new play. But he was not destined to finish it.

When for the first time on a June morning of 1960 I looked out of the window of his second floor study in Peredelkino, I saw beyond the grounds a wide, wide stretch of field leading down to the road and over a little stream, up to a hillock with bushes and single trees, to the small village cemetery partly hidden by shrubs. This was the usual view before Boris's eyes when he was working at his desk; but I saw also something he had not seen: from the gate of his house, through the green field, down to the far end of it, there stretched the ribbon of a narrow, well defined path, made by thousands of feet on the day of his funeral. It was strange: there had been no announcement on the wireless, not a single obituary in any of the papers, not even a normal official notification of the funeral arrangements; only one tiny inconspicuous notice in the Literary Gazette, to the effect that B. Pasternak had died.

But from the early morning the electric trains arriving from the city brought mourners to Peredelkino; wave after wave of friends and strangers, of local peasants and workmen, of all those to whom Pasternak had meant or was beginning to mean so much, old and young – predominantly young people – were gathering at his house for the final farewell.

How did they know?

The sultry air, the clouds, the whispering leaves must have told them. From house to house, over telephone wires, from mouth to mouth the tragic news spread over the whole of Russia. The very silence shouted it. A handwritten message with the time of the funeral appeared at the ticket-window of the Moscow-Kiev suburban railway office, and every time it was taken down an identical new one appeared in its place. Train after train, wave upon wave, the spirit of freedom, the conscience of Russia, flocked to Peredelkino to join those already gathered at the house. Richter played Chopin; a sea of spring flowers surrounded the bier.

No use was made of the official van which came to transport the body; the open coffin was carried shoulder high all the long way from the house, over the field, to the road, over the stream and up to the three tall pine trees on the hillside. This was where he wanted to be buried. There he lies, and the picturesque pine trees look far over the stretch of fields to his distant home, at his window. It is from this hillside that for years, at the approach of winter, Boris thought his death was staring at him, as he described it in one of his poems.

Boris Pasternak died on the 30th May, fifteen years after his father, almost to the day; Leonid Pasternak had lived until the morning of the 31st.

FEBRUARY

Black spring! Pick up your pen, and weeping,
Of February, in sobs and ink,
Write poems, while the slush in thunder
Is burning in the black of spring.

Through clanking wheels, through church bells ringing
A hired cab will take you where
The town has ended, where the showers
Are louder still than ink and tears.

Where rooks, like charred pears, from the branches
In thousands break away, and sweep
Into the melting snow, instilling
Dry sadness into eyes that weep.

Beneath—the earth is black in puddles,
The wind with croaking screeches throbs,
And—the more randomly, the surer
Poems are forming out of sobs.

VENICE

A click of window glass had roused me
Out of my sleep at early dawn.
Beneath me Venice swam in water,
A sodden pretzel made of stone.

It was all quiet now; however,
While still asleep, I heard a cry—
And like a sign that had been silenced
It still disturbed the morning sky.

It hung—a trident of the Scorpion—
Above the sleeping mandolins
And had been uttered by an angry
Insulted woman's voice, maybe.

Now it was silent. To the handle
Its fork was stuck in morning haze.
The Grand Canal, obliquely grinning
Kept looking back—a runaway.

Reality was born of dream-shreds
Far off, among the hired boats.
Like a Venetian woman, Venice
Dived from the bank to glide afloat.

SPRING
(fragment 3)

Is it only dirt you notice?
Does the thaw not catch your glance?
As a dapple-grey fine stallion
Does it not through ditches dance?

Is it only birds that chatter
In the blueness of the skies,
Sipping through the straws of sunrays
Lemon liturgies on ice?

Only look, and you will see it:
From the rooftops to the ground
Moscow, all day long, like Kitezh
Lies, in light-blue water drowned.

Why are all the roofs transparent
And the colours crystal-bright?
Bricks like rushes gently swaying,
Mornings rush into the night.

Like a bog the town is swampy
And the scabs of snow are rare.
February, like saturated
Cottonwool in spirits, flares.

This white flame wears out the garrets,
And the air, in the oblique
Interlace of twigs and birds, is
Naked, weightless and unique.

In such days the crowds of people
Knock you down; you are unknown,
Nameless; and your girl is with them,
But you, too, are not alone.

THE SWIFTS

The swifts have no strength any more to retain,
To check the light-blue evening coolness.
It burst from their breasts, from their throats, under strain
And flows out of hand in its fullness.

There is not a thing that could stop them, up there,
From shrilly, exultedly crying,
Exclaiming: The earth has made off to nowhere,
O look! It has vanished—O triumph!

As cauldrons of water are ended in steam
When quarrelsome bubbles are rising—
Look—there is no room for the earth—from the seam
Of the gorge to the drawn-out horizon!

THREE VARIANTS

1

When in front of you hangs the day with its
Smallest detail—fine or crude—
The intensely hot cracking squirrel-sounds
Do not cease in the resinous wood.

The high line of pine-trees stands asleep,
Drinking in and storing strength,
And the wood is peeling and drip by drip
Is shedding freckled sweat.

2

From miles of calm the garden sickens,
The stupor of the angered glen
Is more alarming than an evil
Wild storm, a frightful hurricane.

The garden's mouth is dry, and smells of
Decay, of nettles, roofing, fear . . .
The cattle's bellowing is closing
Its ranks. A thunderstorm is near.

3

On the bushes grow the tatters
Of disrupted clouds; the garden
Has its mouth full of damp nettles:
Such—the smell of storms and treasures.

Tired shrubs are sick of sighing.
Patches in the sky increase. The
Barefoot blueness has the gait of
Cautious herons in the marshes.

And they gleam, like lips that glisten,
When the hand forgets to wipe them:
Supple willow-switches, oak-leaves,
And the hoofprints by the horsepond.

ON THE STEAMER

The stir of leaves, the chilly morning air
Were like delirium; half awake
Jaws clamped; the dawn beyond the Kama glared
Blue, as the plumage of a drake.

There was a clattering of crockery,
A yawning steward taking stock,
And in the depth, as high as candlesticks,
Within the river, glow-worms flocked.

They hung from streets along the waterfront,
A scintillating string; it chimed
Three times; the steward with a napkin tried
To scratch away some candle grime.

Like a grey rumour, crawling from the past,
A mighty epic of the reeds,
With ripples in the beads of street lamps, fast
Towards Perm the Kama ran upon a breeze.

Choking on waves, and almost drowning, but
Still swimming on beyond the boat
A star kept diving and resurfacing
An icon's shining light afloat.

A smell of paint mixed with the galley smells,
And on the Kama all along,
The twilight drifted, secrets gathering,
With not a splash it drifted on . . .

A glass in hand, your pupils narrowing
You watched the slips of tongue perform
A whirling play on words, at suppertime,
But were not drawn into their swarm.

You called your partner to old happenings,
To waves of days before your day,
To plunge in them, a final residue
Of the last drop, and fade away.

The stir of leaves in chilly morning air
Was like delirium; half awake
One yawned; the east beyond the Kama glared
Blue, as the plumage of a drake.

And, like a bloodbath now the morning came,
A flaming flood of oil—to drown
The steamer's gaslights in the stateroom and
The waning street lamps of the town.

TO THE MEMORY OF DEMON

Used to come in the blue
Of the glacier, at night, from Tamara.
With his wingtips he drew
Where the nightmares should boom, where to bar them.

Did not sob, nor entwine
The denuded, the wounded, the ailing. . . .
A stone slab has survived
By the Georgian church, at the railings.

Hunchback shadows, distressed,
Did not dance by the fence of the temple.
Soft, about the princess
The zurná did not question the lamplight,

But the sparks in his hair
Were aglitter and bursting phosphórous,
And the giant did not hear
The dark Caucasus greying for sorrow.

From the window a step,
'Sleep, beloved', he swore by the burning
Icy peaks (stroking strands of his wrap),
'As a snowslip I will be returning.'

ABOUT THESE POEMS

On winter pavements I will pound
Them down with glistening glass and sun,
Will let the ceiling hear their sound,
Damp corners—read them, one by one.

The attic will repeat my themes
And bow to winter with my lines,
And send leapfrogging to the beams
Bad luck and oddities and signs.

Snow will not monthly sweep and fall
And cover up beginnings, ends.
One day I'll suddenly recall:
The sun exists! Will see new trends,

Will see—the world is not the same;
Then, Christmas jackdaw-like will blink
And with a frosty day explain
What we, my love and I, should think.

The window-halves I'll throw apart,
In muffler from the cold to hide,
And call to children in the yard
'What century is it outside?

Who trod a trail towards the door,
The hole blocked up with sleet and snow,
The while I smoked with Byron or
Was having drinks with Edgar Poe?

While known in Darial or hell
Or armoury, as friend, I dipped
Like Lermontov's deep thrill, as well
My life in vermouth as my lips.'

NOSTALGIA

To give this book a dedication
The desert sickened,
And lions roared, and dawns of tigers
Took hold of Kipling.

A dried-up well of dreadful longing
Was gaping, yawning.
They swayed and shivered, rubbing shoulders,
Sleek-skinned and tawny.

Since then continuing forever
Their sway in scansion,
They stroll in mist through dewy meadows
Dreamt up by Ganges.

Creeping at dawn in pits and hollows
Cold sunrays fumble.
Funereal, incense-laden dampness
Pervades the jungle.

THE GIRL

From the swing, from the garden, helter-skelter,
A twig runs up to the glass.
Enormous, close, with a drop of emerald
At the tip of the cluster cast.

The garden is clouded, lost in confusion,
In staggering, teeming fuss.
The dear one, as big as the garden, a sister
By nature—a second glass!

But then this twig is brought in a tumbler
And put by the looking-glass;
Which wonders:—Who is it that blurs my vision,
From the dull, from the prison-class?

WET PAINT

'Look out! Wet paint'. My soul was blind,
I have to pay the price,
All marked with stains of calves and cheeks
And hands and lips and eyes.

    I loved you more than luck or grief
    Because with you in sight
    The old and yellowed world became
    As white as painters' white.

I swear my friend, my gloom—it will
One day still whiter gleam,
Than lampshades, than a bandaged brow,
Than a delirious dream.

WITH OARS AT REST

A boat is beating in the breast of the lake.
Willows hang over, tickling and kissing
Neckline and knuckles and rowlocks—O wait,
This could have happened to anyone, listen!

This could be used in a song, to beguile.
This then would mean—the ashes of lilac,
Richness of dew-drenched and crushed camomile,
Bartering lips for a star after twilight.

This is—embracing the firmament; strong
Hercules holding it, clasping still fonder.
This then would mean—whole centuries long
Fortunes for nightingales' singing to squander.

SPRING SHOWER

Winked to the birdcherry, gulped amid tears,
Splashed over carriages' varnish, trees' tremble.
Full moon. The musicians are picking their way
To the theatre. More and more people assemble.

Puddles on stone. Like a throat overfilled
With tears are the roses, deep with wet scalding
Diamonds. Showers of gladness thrill,
Eyelashes, stormclouds, and roses enfolding.

The moon for the first time is casting in plaster
An epic poem uncast till today:
The cordons, the flutter of dresses, the speaker
And people enraptured and carried away.

Whose is the heart whose whole blood shot to glory
Drained from the cheeks? We are held in his grip.
The hands of Kerensky are squeezing together
Into a bunch our aortas and lips.

This is not night, not rain, not a chorus
Of tearing acclaim for him, swelled to a roar —
This is the blinding leap to the Forum
From catacombs wanting an exit before.

It is not roses, not lips, not the roaring
Crowd — it's the surf on Theatre Square,
Marking the end of the long sleep of Europe,
Proud of her own reawakening here.

IMITATORS

A boat came in; the cliff was baked;
The noisy boat-chain fell and clanked on
The sand—an iron rattle-snake,
A rattling rust among the plankton.

And two got out; and from the cliff
I felt like calling down, 'Forgive me,
But would you kindly throw yourselves
Apart or else into the river?

Your miming is without a fault—
Of course the seeker finds the fancied—
But stop this playing with the boat!
Your model on the cliff resents it.'

SULTRY NIGHT

It drizzled, but not even grasses
Would bend within the bag of storm;
Dust only gulped its rain in pellets,
The iron roof – in powder form.

The village did not hope for healing.
Deep as a swoon the poppies yearned
Among the rye in inflammation,
And God in fever tossed and turned.

In all the sleepless, universal,
The damp and orphaned latitude,
The sighs and moans, their posts deserting,
Fled with the whirlwind in pursuit.

Behind them ran blind slanting raindrops
Hard on their heels, and by the fence
The wind and dripping branches argued –
My heart stood still – at my expense.

I felt this dreadful garden chatter
Would last forever, since the street
Would also notice me, and mutter
With bushes, rain and window shutter.

No way to challenge my defeat –
They'd argue, talk me off my feet.

THUNDERSTORM,
INSTANTANEOUS FOREVER

After this the halt and summer
Parted company; and taking
Off his cap at night the thunder
Took a hundred blinding stills.

Lilac clusters faded; plucking
Off an armful of new lightnings,
From the field he tried to throw them
At the mansion in the hills.

And when waves of evil laughter
Rolled along the iron roofing
And, like charcoal on a drawing,
Showers thundered on the fence,

Then the crumbling mind began to
Blink; it seemed it would be floodlit
Even in those distant corners
Where the light is now intense.

STARS WERE RACING

Stars were racing; waves were washing headlands.
Salt went blind, and tears were slowly drying.
Darkened were the bedrooms; thoughts were racing,
And the Sphinx was listening to the desert.

Candles swam. It seemed that the Colossus'
Blood grew cold; upon his lips was spreading
The blue shadow smile of the Sahara.
With the turning tide the night was waning.

Sea-breeze from Morocco touched the water.
Simooms blew. In snowdrifts snored Archangel.
Candles swam; the rough draft of 'The Prophet'
Slowly dried, and dawn broke on the Ganges.

ILLNESS

The patient watches. Six days long
In frenzy blizzards rave relentlessly,
Roll over rooftops, roar along,
Brace, rage, and fall, collapsing senselessly.

In snowstorms Christmas is consumed.
He dreams: they came and lifted someone.
He starts: "Whom? Me?" There was a call,
A tolling bell . . . Not New Year's summons?

Far, in the Kremlin, booms Ivan,[1]
Dives, drowns, resounds in swaying motion.
He sleeps. When great, a blizzard can
Be called Pacific, as the Ocean.

THE PATIENT'S SWEATER

A life of its own and a long one is led
By this penguin, with nothing to do with the breast—
The wingless pullover, the patient's old vest;
Now pass it some warmth, move the lamp to the bed.

It dreams of the skiing; in darkness it poured
From shaftbows, from harness, from bodies; it seemed
That Christmas itself also sweated and snored;
The walking, the riding—all squeaked and all steamed.

A homestead, and horror and bareness beside,
Cut-glass in the sideboards, and carpets and chests;
The house was inflamed; this attracted the fence;
The lights swam in pleurisy, seen from outside.

Consumed by the sky, bloated shrubs on the way
Were white as a scare and had ice in their looks.
The blaze from the kitchen laid down by the sleigh
On the snow the enormous hands of the cooks.

YOU ARE DISAPPOINTED?
(from 'The Break' section 6)

You are disappointed? You thought that in peace we
Would part to the sound of a requiem, a swan-song?
You counted on grief, with your pupils dilated,
Their invincibility trying in tears on?

At the mass from the vaults then the murals had crumbled,
By the play on the lips of Sebastian shaken. . . .
But tonight to my hatred all seems drawn-out dawdling,
What a pity there is not a whip for my hatred!

In darkness, collecting its wits instantaneously,
It knew without thinking: it would plough it over—
That it's time; that a suicide would be superfluous;
That this too would have been of a tortoise-like slowness.

From "BEFORE THE WINTER"

The spring – it had simply been you,
And so, to a certain extent,
The summer; but autumn – this scandalous blue
Of wallpaper? Rubbish and felt?

They lead an old horse to the knacker's yard.
His wistful, short-breathing nostrils
Are listening: wet camomile and moss,
Or maybe a whiff of horsemeat.

Imbibe with your lips and the blaze of your eyes
The transparent days' tear-stained vagueness,
Like the drift of an empty bottle of scent,
Its nostalgic lingering fragrance.

To sleep, not to argue. Despairingly
To sleep. Not to open the window
Where last summer, in frenzy, July
Was burning and glowing like jasper,
And melting the glass, and was pairing
The same crimson dragonflies,
Which now, on their nuptial beds,
Are deader and more transparent
Than crumbled dry cigarettes.

How sleepy and chilly are windows
In the twilight hours of frost.
Dry vitriol oil.[2] At the bottom,
A gnat, and expired wasps.

How draughty the north is. How ruffled
And sulky . . . O whirlwind, drive,
Feel, search all the crannies and hollows,
Find me my song alive!

HERE A RIDDLE . . .

Here a riddle has drawn a strange nailmark. To sleep now!
I'll reread, understand with the light of the sun,
But until I am wakened, to touch the beloved
As I do has been given to none.

How I touched you! So touched were you even by the copper
Of my lips, as an audience is touched by a play,
And the kiss was like summer; it lingered and lingered,
Only later the thunderstorm came.

And I drank in long draughts, like the birds, half-unconscious.
The stars trickle slowly through the throat to the crop,
While the nightingales roll up their eyes in a shudder
From the firmament draining the night drop by drop.

THE ZOO

The zoo lies in the parkland thickets.
We enter and hold out our tickets
To park attendants who surround
The entrance-arch; and look around.

Here through the gates in grotto fashion
We now encounter in succession
Huge limestone mouldings, and beyond—
The wind-swept silver-surfaced pond,
Throughout peculiarly aquiver,
Seized with an abstract fever-shiver.

Now mixing with haphazard sounds,
The puma's distant roar resounds
All through the park; this far-off roaring
Rolls on like thunder skyward soaring,
Exciting, menacing, and loud—
But there is not a single cloud!

With a good-neighbourly appearance
The children chat with brown-bear parents;
The ringing slabs are damped, one feels,
By thumping bear-cubs' naked heels.

Here, after their exhaustive sunning,
Into their swimming-pool are running
Child, father, mother polar-bear,
In nothing but their underwear.
This trio splashes, roars and pants,
But does not lose the beltless pants,
And no amount of washing betters
The soiled and shaggy trouser-tatters.

Prior to dirtying, the vixen
Will look askance and sniff, then fix on
The chosen spot. Avid and lanky,

Their bark like padlocks sharp and clanky,
The wolves are famished in their greed;
Their eyes are full of dried-up heat.
The snapping mother-wolf is stung
By children laughing at her young.

A lioness, the people facing,
Relentlessly the floorboards pacing
And turning on her only track
First there, then back, then there, then back,
Is driven by her very raging
When brushing at the iron caging;
The barrier pattern stark and black,
Is moving with her there and back.

The self same iron pattern sends a
Bewildered panther into frenzy.

The same recurring bars again
Will chase a cheetah on a chain.

More lady-like than any lady
The llama looks when promenading;
She curtseys, spits into your face,
And leaps away with haughty grace.

The desert ship observes with sadness
This shallow act of sudden madness.
The camel's reasoning is wise:
'One does not spit in grown-ups' eyes!'
All round him human waves are surging,
And out of them he is emerging
With his steep rounded camel's breast—
A rowing boat upon a crest.

The garb of guinea-fowl and pheasants
Is brightest Sunday-best of peasants
Here tinsel, steel and silver thread
Are glittering as they are shed.

The peacock: seeing is believing.
A shot-silk shawl of blue-black weaving
He wears, a hot and sooty sight.
He walks, mysterious as night,
Extinguished now behind a turning,
Now once again in splendour burning,
Emerging from behind a fence,
His tail like skies at night immense,
With falling stars defying counting,
Of falling stars a playing fountain.

The parrots push away their trough,
They've had a snack and had enough;
They peck one grain and feel they must
Rub clean their beaks in sheer disgust.
Perhaps because of jokes they crack,
Their tongues like coffee-beans are black.
Some of their family have feathers
Like Persian lilac; some, one gathers,
In error classed as birds, instead
Should blossom on a flower bed.

The scarlet-bottomed great attraction,
The grey baboon is seen in action.
The public seem to like him best.
By quiet lunacy possessed
He either lingers, grinning, baring
His teeth, or suddenly, a daring
Gymnast, into the air he flings
And from the lofty branches swings,
Intent on making an impression.
Or on all fours in poodle fashion
He runs around; or in a twist
Scratches his cheekbone with a fist;
Or else again, as monkeys should,
He pesters you and begs for food.

In a thick-sided tub, decaying,
Lie pickled guts—the notice saying

That this is mud with a reptile:
A young Egyptian crocodile.
He does not look at all aggressive;
When grown he may be more impressive.

By-passing on our way some cages,
Stopping at others, thus in stages
We follow notices which lead
Us 'To The Elephants': Indeed
Here is the drowsy mass, ascending
Up to the beams, a cartload standing
Within a warehouse, and a flock
Of hay is whirling on the block.
The monster turns around thereafter,
Dislodging block and hay and rafter,
And sweeping up a cloud of husks
Towards the ceiling and the tusks.
His trunk is knitting lofty stitches
Or shuffles over tiles and twitches;
A hoop has made his ankle sore,
He drags a chain along the floor
And something in this dryness hackles:
Perhaps it is the straw that crackles,
Perhaps his ears, patched up and drab,
Like two old aprons of a cab.

Time to return now to the city,
It's getting late, but what a pity!
There still are wonders by the score:
We've seen a third perhaps, no more.

For the last time the tramlines' rumbling
Is mingling with an eagle's grumbling,
And street-noise drowns the lions' roar
Just once again and then—no more.

THE ROUNDABOUTS

Maple leaves were rustling softly
And the East grew rosy-red;
On a perfect summer morning
No-one wants to stay in bed.

Up, we pack in joyful hurry
Apples, sandwiches and buns.
When we name our destination
The full tram takes off at once.

At the terminus another
Tram is waiting for the crowds.
In the distance, whitely gleaming,
We can see the roundabouts.

Waist-deep now in fragrant carpets
Of convolvulus we roll
Down the steep ravine, and scramble
Up the fair-bank one and all.

Swings are there, and games for children,
Flags are flying from a mast,
Wooden horses gallop gaily
Round and round, and raise no dust.

Black their manes and long their horse-tails.
Tail and forelock, fringe and mane
Now are lifted up and floating,
Lowered gently then again,

Lower with each round, and slower,
Slower, slower, slower, stop.
Whirlwinds hide within the roofwork,
Spinning on a centre prop.

Spreading out a spoky circle
The machine is bent with weight;
Strained and burdened the tarpaulin
Tries in vain to fly away.

As if fresh out of a workshop,
Sounding smarter than the click
Of two croquet-balls, the horses
Sharply snap as children kick.

Crowds are milling in the clearing,
Munching, nibbling this and that.
Look—a funny organ-grinder,
Bells adorn his Punch's hat.

Swiftly, deftly, as if sprinkling
Water round him with a mop,
He is shaking all his trinkets,
Lame, he moves without a stop.

And the bells all shake with laughter,
Burst in rapture as they jump,
When the hurdy-gurdy grinder
Drums and knocks and jerks his stump.

Like a trace-horse, neck and body
In an arc he steeply bends,
Shifts about and turns the handle,
Rattles on, and claps his hands.

While submerging manes and fringes,
Lace and ribbon and festoon,
Swings and roundabouts are drowning
In the depth of summer noon.

To the roundabouts to meet them,
Rush and lift them in their flight,
Giddy, spinning, joy-infected,
Lime-grove left and duck-pond right.

Steep the turning from the cross-roads
To the horse-rides. In delight
Children gallop, whirling, greeting
Lime-grove left and duck-pond right.

Vanished now, again returning,
Past they rush and back in sight,
And they keep and keep recurring:
Lime-grove left and duck-pond right.

Whirlwinds fill the roof-umbrella
Spinning on a centre-prop;
Slower circles the propeller,
Slower, slower, slower, stop.

TO A FRIEND

Do I not know that groping in the dimness
The darkness would have never found the sun?
Do I, a freak, feel happiness of millions
No closer than the happiness of some?

Does not the Five-Year Plan assess and score us,
And do I with it, too, not rise and fall?
But what am I to do about my thorax,
And that which is the sluggishest of all?

How pointless in the days of the Great Soviet,
Where strongest passions are assigned a place,
To have a vacancy left over for the poet:
It's dangerous if not an empty space.

HERE WILL BE ECHOES . . .
(from 'Waves', fragment 4)

Here will be echoes in the mountains,
The distant landslides' rumbling boom,
The rocks, the dwellings in the village,
The sorry little inn, the gloom

Of something black beyond the Terek,
Clouds moving heavily. Up there
The day was breaking very slowly;
It dawned, but light was nowhere near.

One sensed the heaviness of darkness
For miles ahead around Kazbek
Wound on the heights: though some were trying
To throw the halter from their neck.

As if cemented in an oven,
In the strange substance of a dream,
A pot of poisoned food, the region
Of Daghestan there slowly steamed.

Its towering peaks towards us rolling,
All black from top to foot, it strained
To meet our car, if not with clashing
Of daggers, then with pouring rain.

The mountains were preparing trouble.
The handsome giants, fierce and black,
Each one more evil than the other
Were closing down upon our track.

Sometime at a concert hall, in recollection,
A Brahms intermezzo will wound me – I'll start,
Remember that summer, the flowerbed garden,
The walks and the bathing, the tryst of six hearts,

The awkward, shy artist, with steep, dreamlike forehead,
Her smile, into which one would dive for a while,
A smile, as good natured and bright as a river,
Her artist's appearance, her forehead, her smile.

They'll play me some Brahms – I will shudder, surrender,
And in retrospection the sounds will evoke
That faraway summer, the hoard of provisions,
My son and my brother, the garden, the oak.

The artist would stuff in her overall pockets
Her pencils, and objects with fanciful names,
Or would, inadvertently dropping her palette,
Turn much of the grass into colourful stains.

They'll play me some Brahms – I'll surrender, remember
The stubborn dry brushwood, the entrance, the roof,
Her smile and appearance, the mouth and the eyebrows,
The darkened verandah, the steps and the rooms.

And suddenly, as in a fairytale sequence,
The family, neighbours and friends will appear,
And – memories crowding – I'll drown in my weeping
Before I have time to have shed all my tears.

And, circling around in a swift intermezzo –
Embracing the song like a treetrunk at noon,
Four families' shadows will turn on the meadow
To Brahms's compelling and childhood-clear tune.

O HAD I KNOWN . . .

O had I known that thus it happens,
When first I started, that at will
Your lines with blood in them destroy you,
Roll up into your throat and kill,

My answer to this kind of joking
Had been a most decisive 'no'.
So distant was the start, so timid
The first approach—what could one know?

But older age is Rome, demanding
From actors not a gaudy blend
Of props and reading, but in earnest
A tragedy, with tragic end.

A slave is sent to the arena
When feeling has produced a line.
Then breathing soil and fate take over
And art has done and must resign.

FROM EARLY DAWN . . .

From early dawn the thirtieth of April
Is given up to children of the town,
And caught in trying on the festive necklace,
By dusk it only just is settling down.

Like heaps of squashy berries under muslin
The town emerges out of crimson gauze.
Along the streets the boulevards are dragging
Their twilight with them, like a rank of dwarves.

The evening world is always eve and blossom,
But this one with a sprouting of its own
From May-day anniversaries will flower
One day into a commune fully blown.

For long it will remain a day of shifting,
Pre-festive cleaning, fanciful décor,
As once it used to be with Whitsun birches
Or pan-Athenian fires long before.

Just so they will go on, conveying actors
To their assembly points; beat sand; just so
Pull up towards illuminated ledges
The plywood boards, the crimson calico.

Just so in threes the sailors briskly walking
Will skirt the grass in gardens and in parks,
The moon at nightfall sink into the pavements
Like a dead city or a burnt-out hearth.

But with each year more splendid and more spreading
The taut beginning of the rose will bloom,
More clearly grow in health and sense of honour,
Sincerity more visibly will loom.

The living folksongs, customs and traditions
Will ever spreading, many-petalled lay
Their scent on fields and industries and meadows
From early buddings on the first of May,

Until the full fermented risen spirit
Of ripened years will shoot up, like the smell
Of humid centifolia. It will have to
Reveal itself, it cannot help but tell.

CRAFT

When, having finished, I shall move my armchair,
The page will gasp, awakened from the strain.
Delirious, she[3] is half asleep at present,
Obedient to suspense and to the rain.

The heaviness of burnt-out ships has numbed her,
Prostrated, weighted down her senseless form;
You cannot dupe this one by false pretences –
It is the poet who will keep her warm.

I told her at an hour (its secret shudder
Vouchsafed by fancy) when the winter will
Light up green screeching ice, fed up with waiting
Behind an office worker's window sill,

And clocks in banks and other public places,
While drinking in the snow and outside's dark,
Will suddenly jump up and strike – their faces
Crossed by the clockhands at the "seven" mark –

At such a deep, at such a fateful hour,
I made the page wake up and take her chance,
To put on hood and scarf, and venture out to
Descendants, strangers, shaking off her trance.

THE ARTIST

Humble home. But rum, and charcoal
Grog of sketches on the wall,
And the cell becomes a mansion,
And the garret is a hall.

No more waves of housecoats: questions,
Even footsteps disappear;
Glassy mica fills the latticed
Work-encompassed vault of air.

Voice, commanding as a levy,
Does not leave a thing immune,
Smelting, fusing . . . In his gullet
Flows the tin of molten spoons.

What is fame for him, and glory,
Name, position in the world,
When the sudden breath of fusion
Blends his words into the Word?

He will burn for it his chattels,
Friendship, reason, daily round.
On his desk – a glass, unfinished,
World forgotten, clock unwound.

Clustered stanzas change like seething
Wax at fortune-telling times.[4]
He will bless the sleeping children
With the steam of molten rhymes.

FALSE ALARM

From early morning—nonsense
With tubs and troughs and strain,
With dampness in the evening
And sunsets in the rain.

Deep sighing of the darkness
And choking swallowed tears,
A railway-engine's calling
Down from the sixteenth verst.

Outside and in the garden
A short fast-darkening day;
Small breakages and losses
In true September way.

In daytime autumn's vastness
Beyond the stream is rent
By wailing in the graveyard,
By anguish and lament.

But when the widow's sobbing
Is carried from the bank,
With all my blood I'm with her
And see my death point-blank.

As every year I see it
Out of the hall downstairs,
The long-delayed approaching
Of this my final year.

Through leaves in yellow terror,
Its way swept clear, I see
That winter from the hillside
Is staring down at me.

SPRING 1944

This spring the world is new and different;
More lively is the sparrows' riot.
I do not even try expressing it,
How full my soul is and how quiet.

I think and write not as I did before;
And with their song of earth, entire
Freed territories add their mighty voice,
A booming octave in a choir.

The breath of spring within our motherland
Is washing off the winter's traces,
Is washing off black rings and crevices
From tear-worn eyes of Slavic races.

The grass is everywhere in readiness;
And ancient Prague, in murk and smother
Still silent, soon will be awakening,
One street more crooked than the other.

Morave and Czech and Jugoslavian
Folk-lores in spring will rise and blossom,
Tearing away the sheet of lawlessness
That winters past have laid across them.

It all will have the haze of fairy tales
Upon it, like the gilt and dazzle
Of ornaments in Boyar chambers and
On the cathedral of St Basil.

A dreamer and a half-night-ponderer,
Moscow I love with all my power.
Here is the source of all the wonderful
With which the centuries will flower.

HAMLET

The murmurs ebb; onto the stage I enter.
I am trying, standing in the door,
To discover in the distant echoes
What the coming years may hold in store.

The nocturnal darkness with a thousand
Binoculars is focused onto me.
Take away this cup, O Abba, Father,
Everything is possible to thee.

I am fond of this thy stubborn project,
And to play my part I am content.
But another drama is in progress,
And, this once, O let me be exempt.

But the plan of action is determined,
And the end irrevocably sealed.
I am alone; all round me drowns in falsehood:
Life is not a walk across a field.

WIND

I am no more but you live on,
And the wind, whining and complaining,
Is shaking house and forest, straining
Not single fir trees one by one
But the whole wood, all trees together,
With all the distance far and wide,
Like sail-less yachts in stormy weather
When moored within a bay they lie.
And this not out of wanton pride
Or fury bent on aimless wronging,
But to provide a lullaby
For you with words of grief and longing.

INTOXICATION

Under osiers with ivy ingrown
We are trying to hide from bad weather.
I am clasping your arms in my own,
In one cloak we are huddled together.

I was wrong. Not with ivy-leaves bound,
But with hops overgrown is the willow.
Well then, let us spread out on the ground
This our cloak as a sheet and a pillow.

FAIRY TALE

Once, in times forgotten,
In a fairy place,
Through the steppe, a rider
Made his way apace.

While he sped to battle,
Nearing from the dim
Distance, a dark forest
Rose ahead of him.

Something kept repeating,
Seemed his heart to graze:
Tighten up the saddle,
Fear the watering-place.

But he did not listen.
Heeding but his will,
At full speed he bounded
Up the wooded hill;

Rode into a valley,
Turning from the mound,
Galloped through a meadow,
Skirted higher ground;

Reached a gloomy hollow,
Found a trail to trace
Down the woodland pathway
To the watering-place.

Deaf to voice of warning,
And without remorse,
Down the slope, the rider
Led his thirsty horse.

– – –

Where the stream grew shallow,
Winding through the glen,
Eerie flames lit up the
Entrance to a den.

Through thick clouds of crimson
Smoke above the spring,
An uncanny calling
Made the forest ring.

And the rider started,
And with peering eye
Urged his horse in answer
To the haunting cry.

Then he saw the dragon,
And he gripped his lance;
And his horse stood breathless
Fearing to advance.

Thrice around a maiden
Was the serpent wound;
Fire-breathing nostrils
Cast a glare around.

And the dragon's body
Moved his scaly neck,
At her shoulder snaking
Whiplike forth and back.

By that country's custom
Was a young and fair
Captive brought as ransom
To the dragon's lair.

This then was the tribute
That the people owed
To the worm—protection
For a poor abode.

Now the dragon hugged his
Victim in alarm,
And the coils grew tighter
Round her throat and arm.

Skyward looked the horseman
With imploring glance,
And for the impending
Fight he couched his lance.

– – –

Tightly closing eyelids.
Heights and cloudy spheres.
Rivers. Waters. Boulders.
Centuries and years.

Helmetless, the wounded
Lies, his life at stake.
With his hooves the charger
Tramples down the snake.

On the sand, together—
Dragon, steed, and lance;
In a swoon the rider,
The maiden—in a trance.

Blue the sky; soft breezes
Tender noon caress.
Who is she? A lady?
Peasant girl? Princess?

Now in joyous wonder
Cannot cease to weep;
Now again abandoned
To unending sleep.

Now, his strength returning,
Opens up his eyes;
Now anew the wounded
Limp and listless lies.

But their hearts are beating.
Waves surge up, die down;
Carry them, and waken,
And in slumber drown.

Tightly closing eyelids.
Heights and cloudy spheres.
Rivers. Waters. Boulders.
Centuries and years.

WINTER NIGHT

It swept, it swept on all the earth,
At every turning,
A candle on the table flared,
A candle, burning.

Like swarms of midges to a flame
In summer weather,
Snowflakes flew up towards the pane
In flocks together.

Snow moulded arrows, rings and stars
The pane adorning.
A candle on the table shone
A candle, burning.

Entangled shadows spread across
The flickering ceiling,
Entangled arms, entangled legs,
And doom, and feeling.

And with a thud against the floor
Two shoes came falling,
And drops of molten candle wax
Like tears were rolling.

And all was lost in snowy mist,
Grey-white and blurring.
A candle on the table stood,
A candle, burning.

The flame was trembling in the draught;
Heat of temptation,
It lifted up two crossing wings
As of an angel.

All February the snow-storm swept.
Each time returning
A candle on the table wept,
A candle burning.

PARTING

A man is standing in the hall
His house not recognizing.
Her sudden leaving was a flight,
Herself, maybe, surprising.

The chaos reigning in the room
He does not try to master.
His tears and headache hide in gloom
The extent of his disaster.

His ears are ringing all day long
As though he has been drinking.
And why is it that all the time
Of waves he keeps on thinking?

When frosty window-panes blank out
The world of light and motion,
Despair and grief are doubly like
The desert of the ocean.

She was as dear to him, as close
In all her ways and features,
As is the seashore to the wave,
The ocean to the beaches.

As over rushes, after storm
The swell of water surges,
Into the deepness of his soul
Her memory submerges.

In years of strife, in times which were
Unthinkable to live in,
Upon a wave of destiny
To him she had been driven,

Through countless obstacles, and past
All dangers never-ended,
The wave had carried, carried her,
Till close to him she'd landed.

And now, so suddenly, she'd left.
What power overrode them?
The parting will destroy them both,
The grief bone-deep corrode them.

He looks around him. On the floor
In frantic haste she'd scattered
The contents of the cupboard, scraps
Of stuff, her sewing patterns.

He wanders through deserted rooms
And tidies up for hours;
Till darkness falls he folds away
Her things into the drawers;

And pricks his finger on a pin
In her unfinished sewing,
And sees the whole of her again,
And silent tears come flowing.

BAD DAYS

When Passion week started and Jesus
Came down to the city, that day
Hosannahs burst out at his entry
And palm leaves were strewn in his way.

But days grow more stern and more stormy.
No love can men's hardness unbend;
Their brows are contemptuously frowning,
And now comes the postscript, the end.

Grey, leaden and heavy, the heavens
Were pressing on treetops and roofs.
The Pharisees, fawning like foxes,
Were secretly searching for proofs.

The lords of the Temple let scoundrels
Pass judgement, and those who at first
Had fervently followed and hailed him,
Now all just as zealously cursed.

The crowd on the neighbouring sector
Was looking inside through the gate.
They jostled, intent on the outcome,
Bewildered and willing to wait.

And whispers and rumours were creeping,
Repeating the dominant theme.
The flight into Egypt, his childhood
Already seemed faint as a dream.

And Jesus remembered the desert,
The days in the wilderness spent,
The tempting with power by Satan,
That lofty, majestic descent.

He thought of the wedding at Cana,
The feast and the miracles; and
How once he had walked on the waters
Through mist to a boat, as on land;

The beggarly crowd in a hovel,
The cellar to which he was led;
How, startled, the candle-flame guttered,
When Lazarus rose from the dead . . .

MARY MAGDALENE (I)

As soon as night descends, we meet.
Remorse my memories releases.
The demons of the past compete,
And draw and tear my heart to pieces,
Sin, vice and madness and deceit,
When I was slave of men's caprices
And when my dwelling was the street.

The deathly silence is not far;
A few more moments only matter,
Which the Inevitable bar.
But at the edge, before they scatter,
In front of thee my life I shatter,
As though an alabaster jar.

O what might not have been my fate
By now, my teacher and my saviour,
Did not eternity await
Me at the table, as a late
New victim of my past behaviour!

But what can sin now mean to me,
And death, and hell, and sulphur burning,
When, like a graft onto a tree,
I have—for everyone to see—
Grown into being part of thee
In my immeasurable yearning?

When pressed against my knees I place
Thy precious feet, and weep, despairing,
Perhaps I'm learning to embrace
The cross's rough four-sided face;
And, fainting, all my being sways
Towards thee, thy burial preparing.

IT IS NOT SEEMLY

It is not seemly to be famous:
Celebrity does not exalt;
There is no need to hoard your writings
And to preserve them in a vault.

To give your all—this is creation,
And not—to deafen and eclipse.
How shameful, when you have no meaning,
To be on everybody's lips!

Try not to live as a pretender,
But so to manage your affairs
That you are loved by wide expanses,
And hear the call of future years.

Leave blanks in life, not in your papers,
And do not ever hesitate
To pencil out whole chunks, whole chapters
Of your existence, of your fate.

Into obscurity retiring
Try your development to hide,
As autumn mist on early mornings
Conceals the dreaming countryside.

Another, step by step, will follow
The living imprint of your feet;
But you yourself must not distinguish
Your victory from your defeat.

And never for a single moment
Betray your *credo* or pretend,
But be alive—this only matters—
Alive and burning to the end.

SOUL

My mournful soul, you, sorrowing
For all my friends around,
You have become the burial vault
Of all those hounded down.

Devoting to their memory
A verse, embalming them,
In torment, broken, lovingly
Lamenting over them,

In this our mean and selfish time,
For conscience and for quest
You stand – a columbarium
To lay their souls to rest.

The sum of all their agonies
Has bowed you to the ground.
You smell of dust, of death's decay,
Of morgue and burial mound.

My beggarly, dejected soul,
You heard and saw your fill;
Remembered all and mixed it well,
And ground it like a mill.

Continue pounding and compound
All that I witnessed here
To graveyard compost, as you did
For almost forty years.

CHANGE

I used to glorify the poor,
Not simply lofty views expressing:
Their lives alone, I felt, were true,
Devoid of pomp and window dressing.

No stranger to the manor house,
Its finery and lordly tenor,
I was a friend of down-and-outs,
And shunned the idly sponging manner.

For choosing friendship in the ranks
Of working people, though no rebel,
I had the honour to be stamped
As also one among the rabble.

The state of basements, unadorned,
Of attics with no frills or curtains
Was tangible without pretence
And full of substance, weighty, certain.

And I went bad when rot defaced
Our time, and life became infested,
When grief was censured as disgrace
And all played optimists and yes-men.

My faith in those who seemed my friends
Was broken and our ties were sundered.
I, too, lost Man, the Human, since
He had been lost by all and sundry.

JULY

A ghost is roaming through the building,
And shadows in the attic browse;
Persistently intent on mischief
A goblin roams about the house.

He gets into your way, he fusses,
You hear his footsteps overhead,
He tears the napkin off the table
And creeps in slippers to the bed.

With feet unwiped he rushes headlong
On gusts of draught into the hall
And whirls the curtain, like a dancer,
Towards the ceiling, up the wall.

Who is this silly mischief-maker,
This phantom and this double-face?
He is our guest, our summer lodger,
Who spends with us his holidays.

Our house is taken in possession
By him, while he enjoys a rest.
July, with summer air and thunder—
He is our temporary guest.

July, who scatters from his pockets
The fluff of blow-balls in a cloud,
Who enters through the open window,
Who chatters to himself aloud,

Unkempt, untidy, absent-minded,
Soaked through with smell of dill and rye,
With linden-blossom, grass and beet-leaves,
The meadow-scented month July.

THE LINDEN AVENUE

A house of unimagined beauty
Is set in parkland, cool and dark;
Gates with an arch; then meadows, hillocks,
And oats and woods beyond the park.

Here, with their crowns each other hiding,
Enormous linden trees engage
In dusky, quiet celebration
Of their two hundred years of age.

And underneath their vaulted branches,
Across the regularly drawn
Symmetric avenues, grow flowers
In flower-beds upon a lawn.

Beneath the trees, on sandy pathways,
Not one bright spot relieves the dark,
Save—like an opening in a tunnel—
The distant entrance of the park.

But now the blossom-time is starting,
The walled-in linden trees reveal
And spread about within their shadow
Their irresistible appeal.

The visitors, in summer clothing,
While walking on the crunchy sand,
Breathe in unfathomable fragrance
Which only bees can understand.

This gripping scent is theme and subject,
Whereas—however well they look—
The flower-beds, the lawn, the garden,
Are but the cover of a book.

The clustered, wax-bespattered flowers
On massive trees, sedate and old,
Lit up by raindrops, burn and sparkle
Above the mansion they enfold.

AUTUMN FROST

The morning sun shows like a pillar
Of fire through smoke on frosty days.
As on a faulty snap, it cannot
Make out my features in the haze.

The distant trees will hardly see me
Until the sun at last can break
Out of the fog, and flash triumphant
Upon the meadows by the lake.

A passer-by in mist receding
Is recognized when he has passed.
You walk on hoarfrost-covered pathways
As though on mats of plaited bast.

The frost is covered up in gooseflesh,
The air is false like painted cheeks,
The earth is shivering, and sick of
Breathing potato-stalks for weeks.

WHEN IT CLEARS UP

The lake is like a giant saucer;
Beyond—a gathering of clouds;
Like stern and dazzling mountain-ranges
Their massif the horizon crowds.

And with the light that swiftly changes,
The landscape never stays the same.
One moment clad in sooty shadows,
The next—the woods are all aflame.

When, after days of rainy weather,
The heavy curtain is withdrawn,
How festive is the sky, burst open!
How full of triumph is the lawn!

The wind dies down, the distance lightens,
And sunshine spreads upon the grass;
The steaming foliage is translucent
Like figures in stained-window glass.

Thus from the church's narrow windows
In glimmering crowns, on spreading wings
Gaze into time in sleepless vigil
Saints, hermits, prophets, angels, kings.

The whole wide world is a cathedral;
I stand inside, the air is calm,
And from afar at times there reaches
My ear the echo of a psalm.

World, Nature, Universe's Essence,
With secret trembling, to the end,
I will thy long and moving service
In tears of happiness attend.

NIGHT

The night proceeds and dwindling
Prepares the day's rebirth.
An airman is ascending
Above the sleeping earth.

And almost disappearing
In cloud, a tiny spark,
He now is like a cross-stitch,
A midget laundry-mark.

Beneath him are strange cities,
And heavy traffic-lanes,
And night-clubs, barracks, stokers,
And railways, stations, trains.

The shadow of his wing-span
Falls heavy on the cloud.
Celestial bodies wander
Around him in a crowd.

And there, with frightful listing
Through emptiness, away
Through unknown solar systems
Revolves the Milky Way.

In limitless expanses
Are headlands burning bright.
In basements and in cellars
The stokers work all night.

And underneath a rooftop
In Paris, maybe Mars
Or Venus sees a notice
About a recent farce.

And maybe in an attic
And under ancient slates
A man sits wakeful, working,
He thinks and broods and waits;

He looks upon the planet,
As if the heavenly spheres
Were part of his entrusted
Nocturnal private cares.

Fight off your sleep: be wakeful,
Work on, keep up your pace,
Keep vigil like the pilot,
Like all the stars in space.

Work on, work on, creator—
To sleep would be a crime—
Eternity's own hostage,
And prisoner of Time.

THE WIND
(4 fragments on Blok, fragment 1)

'The most influential of nitwits,
The sycophant toadies are used
To rule who should live and be lauded
And who should be dead and abused.

Thus no one, maybe, could be certain,
Is Pushkin a poet or not,
Without their elaborate theses
Explaining to us what is what.

But Blok is, thank Heaven, another,
A different matter for once.
He did not descend from Sinai
And did not accept us as sons.

Eternal and not manufactured,
Renowned not according to plan,
Outside schools and systems, he has not
Been foisted upon us by man.

THE ROAD

Down into the ravine, then forward
Up the embankment to the top,
The ribbon of the road runs snaking
Through wood and field without a stop.

By all the precepts of perspective
Well-surfaced highway windings rush
Among the fields, among the meadows,
Not raising dust, nor stuck in slush.

The peaceful pond nearby ignoring
(On which a duck with ducklings swam)
The road once more is forward soaring
On having crossed and left the dam.

Now—down a slope again it hastens,
Now—on and upwards, in a climb,
As only life, maybe, is meant to
Strain up and onward all the time.

Through thousands of unheard-of fancies,
Through times and countries, climb and fall,
Through helps and hindrances it races
Relentless, too, towards a goal;

And this is to have lived your fullest,
Experienced all—at home, abroad—
Just as the landscape now is livened
By twists and turnings of the road.

IN HOSPITAL

They stood, almost blocking the pavement,
As though at a window display;
The stretcher was pushed in position,
The ambulance started away.

Past porches and pavements and people
It plunged with its powerful light
Through streets in nocturnal confusion
Deep into the blackness of night.

The headlights picked out single faces,
Militiamen, stretches of street.
The nurse with a smelling-salts phial
Was rocked to and fro on her seat.

A drain gurgled drearily. Cold rain
Was falling. The hospital-clerk
Took out a fresh form of admission
And filled it in, mark upon mark.

They gave him a bed by the entrance;
No room in the ward could be found.
Strong iodine vapour pervaded
The draught from the windows around.

His window framed part of the garden,
And with it a bit of the sky.
The newcomer studied the floorboards,
The ward and the objects nearby,

When, watching the nurse's expression
Of doubt, in her questioning drive,
He suddenly knew this adventure
Would hardly release him alive.

Then, grateful, he turned to the window
Behind which the wall, further down,
Was breathing like smouldering tinder,
Lit up by the glare of the town.

There, far off the city was glowing
All crimson-aflame; in its swell
A maple-branch, ragged, was bowing
To bid him a silent farewell.

'O Lord', he was thinking, 'how perfect
Thy works are, how perfect and right;
The walls and the beds and the people,
This death-night, the city at night!

'I drink up a sedative potion,
And weeping, my handkerchief trace.
O Father, the tears of emotion
Prevent me from seeing thy face.

'Dim light scarcely touches my bedstead.
It gives me such comfort to drift
And feel that my life and my lot are
Thy priceless and wonderful gift.

'While dying in fading surroundings
I feel how thy hands are ablaze,
The hands that have made me and hold me
And hide like a ring in a case.'

MUSIC

The block of flats loomed towerlike.
Two sweating athletes, human telpher,
Were carrying up narrow stairs,
As though a bell onto a belfry,

As to a stony tableland
The tables of the law, with caution,
A huge and heavy concert-grand,
Above the city's restless ocean.

At last it stands on solid ground,
While deep below the din and clatter
Are damped, as though the town were drowned –
Sunk to the bottom of a legend.

The tenant of the topmost flat
Looks down on earth over the railings,
As if he held it in his hand,
Its lawful ruler, never failing.

Back in the drawing room he starts
To play – not someone else's music,
But his own thought, a new chorale,
The stir of leaves, Hosannahs booming.

Improvisations sweep and peal,
Bring night, flames, fire barrels rolling,
Trees under downpour, rumbling wheels,
Life of the streets, fate of the lonely . . .

Thus Chopin would, at night, instead
Of the outgrown, naïve and artless,
Write down on the black fretwork stand
His soaring dream, his new departures.

Or, overtaking in their flight
The world by many generations,
Valkyries shake the city roofs
By thunderous reverberations.

Or through the lovers' tragic fate,
Amidst infernal crash and thunder,
Tchaikovsky harrow us to tears,
And rent the concert hall asunder.

AFTER THE INTERVAL

About three months ago, when first
Upon our open, unprotected
And freezing garden snowstorms burst
In sudden fury, I reflected

That I would shut myself away
And in seclusion write a section
Of winter poems, day by day,
To supplement my spring collection.

But nonsense piled up mountain-high,
Like snow-drifts hindering and stifling
And half the winter had gone by,
Against all hopes, in petty trifling.

I understood, alas, too late
Why winter—while the snow was falling,
Piercing the darkness with its flakes—
From outside at my house was calling;

And while with numb white-frozen lips
It whispered, urging me to hurry,
I sharpened pencils, played with clips,
Made feeble jokes and did not worry.

While at my desk I dawdled on
By lamp-light on an early morning,
The winter had appeared and gone—
A wasted and unheeded warning.

FIRST SNOW

Outside the snowstorm spins, and hides
The world beneath a pall.
Snowed under are the paper-girl,
The papers and the stall.

   Quite often our experience
   Has led us to believe
   That snow falls out of reticence,
   In order to deceive.

Concealing unrepentantly
And trimming you in white,
How often he has brought you home
Into the town at night!

   While snowflakes blind and blanket out
   The distance more and more,
   A tipsy shadow gropes his way
   And staggers to the door.

And then he enters hastily . . .
Again, for all I know,
Someone has something sinful to
Conceal in all this snow!

PLOUGHING TIME

What is the matter with the landscape?
Familiar landmarks are not there.
Ploughed fields, like squares upon a chessboard,
Today are scattered everywhere.

The newly-harrowed vast expanses
So evenly are spread about,
As though the valley had been spring-cleaned
Or else the mountains flattened out.

And that same day, in one endeavour,
Outside the furrows every tree
Bursts into leaf, light green and downy,
And stretches skyward, tall and free.

No speck of dust on the new maples,
And colours nowhere are as clean
As is the light-grey of the ploughland
And as the silver-birch's green.

AFTER THE STORM

The air is full of after-thunder freshness,
And everything rejoices and revives.
With the whole outburst of its purple clusters
The lilac drinks the air of paradise.

The gutters overflow; the change of weather
Makes all you see appear alive and new.
Meanwhile the shades of sky are growing lighter,
Beyond the blackest cloud the height is blue.

An artist's hand, with mastery still greater
Wipes dirt and dust off objects in his path.
Reality and life, the past and present,
Emerge transformed out of his colour-bath.

The memory of over half a lifetime
Like swiftly passing thunder dies away.
The century is no more under wardship:
High time to let the future have its say.

It is not revolutions and upheavals
That clear the road to new and better days,
But revelations, lavishness and torments
Of someone's soul, inspired and ablaze.

UNIQUE DAYS

How I remember solstice days
Through many winters long completed!
Each unrepeatable, unique,
And each one countless times repeated.

Of all these days, these only days,
When one rejoiced in the impression
That time had stopped, there grew in years
An unforgettable succession.

Each one of them I can evoke.
The year is to midwinter moving,
The roofs are dripping, roads are soaked,
And on the ice the sun is brooding.

Then lovers hastily are drawn
To one another, vague and dreaming,
And in the heat, upon a tree
The sweating nesting-box is steaming.

And sleepy clock-hands laze away
The clockface wearily ascending.
Eternal, endless is the day,
And the embrace is never-ending.

GOD'S WORLD

Thin as hair are the shadows of sunset
When they follow drawn-out every tree.
On the road through the forest the post-girl
Hands a parcel and letters to me.

By the trail of the cats and the foxes,
By the foxes' and by the cats' trail,
I return with a bundle of letters
To the house where my joy will prevail.

Countries, continents, isthmuses, frontiers,
Lakes and mountains, discussions and news,
Children, grown-ups, old folk, adolescents,
Appreciations, reports and reviews.

O respected and masculine letters!
All of you, none excepted, have brought
A display of intelligent logic
Underneath a dry statement of thought.

Precious, treasured epistles of women!
Why, I also fell down from a cloud.
And eternally now and for ever
To be yours I have solemnly vowed.

Well and you, stamp-collectors, if even
Only one fleeting moment you had
Among us, what a marvellous present
You would find in my sorrowful stead!

NOTES ON THE POEMS

February, p. 27. Why *black* spring? Dirty, thundering slush of the melting snow, black rooks, black ink, black earth in the puddles on the outskirts of the town, 'where the showers are blacker still than ink and tears', says a different version. Many of the lines have been changed many times in the original. The work of the sun used to be helped in Moscow by giant black cauldrons (like those used for heating asphalt), in which the dirty snow was melted down over bonfires in the streets.

Venice, p. 28. Pasternak mentions this poem in his 'Essay in Autobiography as follows: 'for instance, I was writing the poem "Venice" and the poem "The Railway-station". The town on the water stood before me and the circles and figures-of-eight of its reflections swam and multiplied, swelling like a rusk, dipped in tea.... I wanted nothing from myself, from my reader, from the theory of art. I wanted that one poem should contain the town of Venice, and the other—the Brest railway-station'.

Spring, p. 29. Kitezh—a legendary town, sunk in a lake.

To the Memory of Demon, p. 34. 'Demon', one of Lermontov's great poems: the Demon, a banished angel, having experienced everything there is on earth, sick of pleasures and wisdom, of evil and power, glides sad and lonely over the Caucasian mountains. He sees a young Georgian princess, about to be married; falling desperately in love with her, he kills the bridegroom, and appears to Tamara in her dreams; unable to resist him, torn by love and conscience, she flees to a nunnery, but there, too, the Demon pursues her relentlessly with his sincere and dramatic wooing; at last she gives in, and dies from the blaze of his kiss. As he flies away with her soul in his arms, an angel snatches her from him and takes her to Heaven, while the Demon is once again alone. There is a wonderful line in Lermontov's poem about the stone, into which a deep hole had been burnt by a tear, a tear not of human origin. Pasternak loved Lermontov's poetry and dedicated *My*

103

Sister, Life to him. 'To the memory of Demon' is a difficult poem, full of vague allusions and unfinished sentences, leaving it to the reader's imagination to fill in the gaps. (Occasionally this has led to rather comic interpretations.) My line 'The denuded, the wounded, the ailing' reproduces correctly the vagueness of the Russian sentence, where, too, the subject is missing: the Demon's naked arms are meant here, of course. Zurna is a kind of lute. I apologize for my impossible 'phosphórous', but I think it is in keeping with the kind of word-somersaults my brother occasionally performed in his early poems. For the 'snowslip' I owe yet another apology; but both the newest Russian Dictionary of Prof Smirnitsky and the Concise Oxford Dictionary give the word as a legitimate alternative for 'avalanche' (which in its English corruption of the French word sounds terrible to me, and quite out of place in the last line of a lyric poem).

About these Poems, p. 35. Darial—a gorge in the Caucasian Mountains, pierced by the river Terek between vertical walls of rock.

The Girl, p. 37. A pier glass is meant. The idea is that while the branch is still in the garden, and is part of a tree, it is huge, throbbing and alive; but, detached from it, it becomes artificial, dull and hardly noticeable.

Imitators, p. 41. This poem is a sequel to a love poem called 'The Model', but it appears even more connected with the preceding poem 'With oars at rest': the lonely poet on the cliff resents the two lovers' imitations of his and his beloved's past happiness in a boat and on the shore.

Thunderstorm, instantaneous forever, p. 43. Halt = railway-halt. The last two lines of the poem seem illogical, not only in my translation; or does Pasternak mean that not only the dark corners, but also those which already are as light as day would then get brighter still? I have already commented in my Introduction on the interesting rhyme patterns of this poem in the original.

Stars were racing, p. 44. This is one of a series of poems on Pushkin My brother was fascinated by the fact that the greatest Russian poet was of African descent, and Africa, the desert, the Sphinx, and the foaming sea play a great part in my brother's imagery. This particular poem deals with a night in which Pushkin writes his poem 'The Prophet'. The laconic sentences, giving glimpses of this night in various parts of the earth, are very effective in creating an atmosphere of awe and solemnity, and in implying that Pushkin's inspiration is a thing of the same order as a snow-storm, a simoom or the birth of a new day.

Illness, p. 45. 'booms Ivan'. The sound of the bell in the Church of Ivan the Great, in the Kremlin.

The spring – it had simply been you . . . p. 48. 'Dry vitriol oil'. In winter time in Russia one used to put jars with vitriol oil between the two panes of the double windows in order to absorb moisture and prevent them steaming over.

Here will be echoes . . . p. 58. In my translation the first line of the second stanza is not identical with that of the original: my brother's 'Vladikavkaz' is such an unwieldy word in English that I have replaced it with 'Terek', the name of the river in that region, not mentioned in the original. However, this does not change the meaning of the stanza and is geographically correct; the same applies to the next stanza, where I mention the mountain Kasbek by name, contrary to the original, where it is only implied; I think this, too, was legitimate.

From early dawn . . . p. 61. Pan-Athenian fires: torch processions etc. during the Athenian festival.

Craft, p. 63. 'The page will gasp . . . she is half asleep . . .'. As is clear from the whole poem, the author meant the page to be a woman (and not merely because 'page' is of feminine gender in Russian).

The fair copy of this unpublished poem was discovered by T. Superfin in the Manuscript Department of the State Public Library, named after Saltikov-Schedrin. It was inscribed in the album of P. N. Medvedev, and was evidently written in the second half of the twenties. See the 'Russian Page' No. 2 supplement to *Tartu Rüklik Ülikool*, Estonian S.S.R., 26.12.69.

The Artist, p. 64. 'like seething / Wax at fortune-telling times'. In Russia it was the custom to tell fortunes on New Year's Eve by melting wax and pouring it into a bowl of cold water. The shape of the solidified wax was supposed to be the shape of things to come.

Hamlet, p. 67. The last line of the poem is a Russian proverb.

Intoxication, p. 69. The Russian title of this poem is a word which means both 'hops' and 'intoxication'.

The Linden Avenue, p. 84. In the first edition of my book I said in a note to this poem that I recognized the park and the estate described as the country place Molody, where we spent several summers, from 1913 onwards, and where Boris first started to write poetry in earnest. During a recent visit to Moscow, however, I saw there some newly discovered variants of this poem, which prove me to have been wrong: they actually name the place described as the former estate of the Princes Trubetskoy, now a sanatorium of the Academy of Sciences, where my brother spent some time after an illness.

Wind, p. 90. Pasternak, like almost every creative artist, had no patience with the species of crawling literary digesters and commentators who, devoid of any talent of their own, live on (and off) the body of real art and alone have the power to decide on its recognition or destruction. He expresses similar sentiments in his autobiographical essay, in the chapter on Tolstoy's death.

In Hospital, p. 92: See Pasternak's letter to his friend, Nina Tabidze, January 17, 1953: 'Ninochka! I have survived, I am at home. O, how much I have to tell you! . . .
 . . . When this happened and I was taken away, and spent first five evening hours in the admission ward, and then a night in the corridor of an ordinary, huge, overcrowded, municipal hospital, then – in the intervals between loss of consciousness and bouts of nausea and vomiting – I felt such bliss, such tranquility! . . . The mile-long corridor with its sleeping bodies, submerged in quiet and darkness, ended in a window onto the garden, filled with the inky dimness of a rainy night, and the reflected glow of the town, the glare of Moscow, behind the treetops. And this corridor, the heat of the green lampshade on the night-sister's table by the window, the stillness, the shadows of the nurses, and the neighbourhood of death behind the window and behind one's back – the concentration of all this – was such a fathomless, such a superhuman poem!
 At a moment, which seemed to be the last of my life, more than

ever before I longed to talk to God, to praise all I could see, to take it all in, and keep it in me. "Lord" – I whispered – "thank you for laying on the paints so richly, for having made life and death such as they are; for your language which is majesty and music; for having made me an artist, for creativity which is your school, for preparing me – all my life – for this night". And I cried for exultation and happiness.'

BIBLIOGRAPHY

1. *Encounter*, No. 71, August 1959, p. 84.
2. *The New York Times Book Review*, October 29, 1961, p. 50.
3. *Collected Prose Works*, with an introduction by S. Shimansky, Lindsay Drummond, 1945.
4. *Unicorn*, vol. 7, summer 1962.
5. *Poems by Boris Pasternak*, translated by Lydia Slater, Peter Russell, Fairwarp, 1958 and 1959.
6. Ibid., p. 7: '(these translations) will, it is hoped, meet with such a grateful reception that she (Mrs Slater) may be encouraged to give us soon renderings of the bulk of his (Pasternak's) work'.
7. *Twin in the Clouds*, Ed. 'Lirika', Moscow, 1914.
8. *Over the Barriers*, Ed. 'Zentrifuga', Moscow, 1917.
9. *My Sister, Life*, Ed. Grzhebin, Berlin-Petersburg-Moscow, 1922.
10. *Themes and Variations*, Ed. 'Gelikon', Berlin-Moscow, 1923.
11. 'The Roundabouts', GIZ, Leningrad, 1925.
    'The Zoo', GIZ, Moscow, 1929.
12. *Collected Works of Boris Pasternak* (in Russian), University of Michigan Press, 1961, Ed. Gleb Struve and B. Filipoff, introd. by W. Weidle and Countess J. de Proyart.
13. *Second Birth*, Ed. 'Federazia', Moscow, 1932.
14. *On Early Trains*, Ed. 'Sovietsky Pisatel', Moscow, 1943.
15. *The Vastness of Earth*, Ed. 'Sovietsky Pisatel', Moscow, 1945.
16. Cf. also H. Kamen's translations, *In the Interlude*, Oxford University Press, 1962.
17. *Leonid Pasternak*, Ed. Stybel, Warsaw, 1932 (available in the British Museum).
18. *Last Summer* ('Povest'), transl. George Reavey, with an introduction by L. Slater, Penguin Books, 1960.
19. *Safe Conduct, An Early Autobiography, and Other Works*, transl. Alec Brown, Elek Books, London, 1959.
20. *Essay In Autobiography*, transl. Manya Harari, Collins and Harvill Press, London, 1959.
21. *Westermanns Monats-Hefte*, Berlin, November 1932, p. 213.
    The Studio, No. 632, November 1945, London, p. 151.

The Studio, No. 815, March 1961, p. 98.
Iskusstvo, No. 7 p. 65, Moscow, 1961.
Adam, No. 284–286, p. 23, London, 1960.
Der Spiegel, No. 35, August 1962, Hamburg.
Time, August 24, 1962.
Gloucestershire Countryside, February–March 1963, p. 14,
Leamington Spa.